1992

To Ginny

Happy Christmas

from

Eric & Muriel x x

A PICNIC

— WITH —

Mrs BEETON

OUTDOOR FEASTS

A PICNIC
— WITH —
Mrs BEETON

OUTDOOR FEASTS

WARD LOCK

First published 1991 by Ward Lock
Villiers House, 41/47 Strand, London WC2N 5JE, England

A Cassell imprint

British Library Cataloguing in Publication Data
A picnic with Mrs Beeton.
1. Food, History
642.30941

ISBN 0-7063-7036-8

Designed by Cherry Randell
Illustrations by Mike Shoebridge

Typeset in Goudy Old Style by Litho Link Ltd, Welshpool, Powys, Wales

Printed and bound in Gt. Britain by Bath Colourbooks Ltd

1 cup butter = 225 g/8 oz
1 cup caster (superfine) sugar = 200 g/7 oz
1 cup cheese (grated) = 100 g/4 oz
1 cup chicken (chopped) = 150 g/5 oz
1 cup dried fruit = 150 g/5 oz
1 cup flour = 100 g/4 oz
1 cup potatoes (mashed) = 150 g/5 oz
1 cup walnuts (chopped) = 100 g/4oz

◇◇◇◇◇◇◇◇◇◇◇◇◇◇◇◇◇

ONTENTS

INTRODUCTION

The word picnic seems to have entered the English language in about 1748, but there are no clear explanations about its origins. At first, it meant a feast to which all members of the party contributed a dish of some sort. In the early nineteenth century, it came to mean trifling or inconsequential, but soon became associated with outdoor eating parties.

Al fresco celebrations had been popular for hundreds of years, and in the eighteenth century the fashion for elaborate gardens and parks laid out with pavilions, follies, grottoes, temples and arbours, increased the popularity of elegant parties in the fresh air.

Fêtes champêtres were organized in the London pleasure gardens and on private country estates. Guests arrived in fancy dress, brought their own food and settled in some attractive spot to feast and watch the entertainments of fireworks, concerts, dancing and masquerades.

By Queen Victoria's reign, the desire to enjoy the open countryside encouraged expeditions to rugged moorland, archaeological ruins and beauty spots quite far from home. Improved rail services and increased wealth allowed many to experience the pleasure of travel, and picnics became all the rage. On their visits to places of interest, the travelling public usually took their lunch with them, and hampers were filled with elaborate dishes of meat and fish, pies, cakes, wines and spirits.

After Queen Victoria and Prince
Albert discovered Balmoral, much
of their time was spent travelling
into the surrounding hills to shoot,
sketch and walk. Their lunchtime
repast was often eaten in the special
little picnic house that Albert had
built at Feithort. This modest hut
set a trend and earlier classical
pavilions dotted around large
country parks were often replaced
by rustic chalets and thatched
shelters.

Shooting parties also became
very popular among the Victorian
landed gentry. Such outings had
originally been restricted to
farmers, whose lunch would have
been simply bread and cheese.
When gentlemen developed a taste
for the sport, their midday meal
took on the proportions of a
banquet. Silver, china and linen
were sometimes brought from the
main house and laid out on long
trestle tables. Vast quantities of
food were consumed at these five-
course luncheons that often lasted
for about an hour and a half.

Today's picnics can take
advantage of chiller bags, vacuum
flasks, ice packs and airtight
containers so that our meals in the
fresh air are easier to transport and
can be as sumptuous as those
extravagant Victorian repasts.

$\mathcal{S}$OUPS

Since the invention of the vacuum flask, hot soups have become an ideal picnic food. They are easy to carry and deliciously warming. Pack a flask and some sandwiches for a nourishing meal.

HARICOT BEAN AND TOMATO SOUP

175 g/6 oz haricot beans
900 /ml/1½ pints water
*15 g/½ oz butter, margarine **or** bacon fat*
225 g/8 oz tomatoes, sliced
1 onion, sliced
1 carrot, sliced
1 potato, sliced
a bunch of herbs
1 bay leaf
a blade of mace
salt and pepper

Wash the beans and soak in cold water overnight. Drain and put into a saucepan with 900 ml/ 1½ pints water. Bring to the boil, boil rapidly for 10 minutes and then simmer for 50 minutes.

Melt the fat in a pan and fry the vegetables for 10 minutes. Add the fried vegetables to the beans with the herbs, bay leaf and mace. Simmer until the beans are quite soft. Remove the herbs. Rub the soup through a fine sieve or purée in a blender. Reheat, adding salt and pepper to taste. Pour into a vacuum flask for transporting.

SERVES 6

SHOOTING PARTIES

During the autumn and winter, the residents of large Victorian country estates and their guests would form a shooting party and go off for the day to shoot pheasant, deer or grouse. The party included game keepers, gun loaders, beaters, servants, gentlemen and their ladies. A large selection of foods was needed to sustain them through the day. So, a portable meal of stews, casseroles, meat pies and puddings, baked ham, jacket potatoes, vegetables, apple dumplings, steamed puddings, fruit pies, plum cakes, cheeses, beer, cider, gin and brandy was packed into sacks and hot boxes and sent off with the butler and footmen.

Melt the butter in a deep saucepan and in it cook the mushrooms, onion and garlic over a gentle heat for 10 minutes, or until the mushrooms are tender. Keep the lid on the pan and shake it vigorously from time to time. Boil the water or stock, add it to the vegetables with the yeast or meat extract and simmer the whole until the vegetables are quite soft. Remove the mushrooms and chop finely. Purée the onion and liquid in a blender. Mix the milk with the purée, add the mushroom and measure the soup. Blend the flour with cold milk, stock or water and

MUSHROOM CREAM SOUP

50 g/2 oz butter
225 g/8 oz mushrooms
1 onion, chopped
1 garlic clove, crushed
*450 ml/¾ pint water **or** white stock*
*a little yeast **or** meat extract*
450 ml/¾ pint milk
25 g/1 oz plain flour
salt and pepper
150 ml/¼ pint double cream
(optional)
1 egg yolk (optional)

stir it into the soup. Cook the soup until it has thickened and no longer tastes of flour. Add salt and pepper to taste.

After the flour has been cooked, remove the pan from the heat. Mix the egg yolk and cream together, stir them into the soup, which should be well below boiling point. Stir over a gentle heat until the egg yolk thickens, but do not boil. Serve the soup at once; cream and eggs cannot be kept hot.

SERVES 6

CHILDREN'S PICNIC

Scotch eggs
banana sandwiches
plain scones with jam
or
treacle scones
fruit in jelly
moist gingerbread

$\mathscr{P}$IES AND MEATS

Pies and cold meats are easily prepared in advance for a picnic meal. Served with salads, breads, pickles and chutneys, they make a filling and satisfying main course for any occasion.

BOILED HAM

ham
raspings **or** *glaze*
soft dark brown sugar

If the ham has been hung for a long time and is very dry and salty, soak for 24 hours, changing the water as necessary. For most hams about 12 hours' soaking is sufficient.

Clean and trim off the rusty parts.

Put the ham into a saucepan with sufficient cold water to cover and simmer gently until tender, allowing 30 minutes per 450 g/1 lb. When cooked, remove the ham and strip off the skin. Sprinkle the ham with a mixture of equal quantities of raspings and brown sugar. If to be eaten cold, after removing the skin, put the ham back into the water until cold to keep it juicy. Before serving, sprinkle on the raspings and sugar, or glaze, if preferred.

Note To ensure that the ham is sweet insert a sharp knife close to the bone – when withdrawn there should be no unpleasant smell.

B R A W N

a pig's head weighing about
2.75 kg/6 lb
30 ml/2 tbsp salt
1.25 ml/¼ tsp ground cloves
a pinch of ground mace
675 g/1½ lb lean beef
5 ml/1 tsp pepper
1 onion

Clean the head well and soak in water for 2 hours. Put in a saucepan with the remaining ingredients and almost cover with cold water. Boil for about 3 hours or until quite tender. Take out the head and remove all the flesh. Put the bones back into the liquid and boil quickly until well reduced so that it will form a jelly when cold.

Roughly chop the meat with a sharp knife, work quickly to prevent the fat settling in and put into a wet mould, basin or cake tin. Pour some of the hot liquid over the meat through a strainer. Leave until quite cold and turn out when it has set.

Note The liquor in which the meat was cooked will make excellent soup, and the fat, if skimmed off and clarified well, will answer the purposes of lard.

SERVES 6

DEVILLED TURKEY LEGS

2 turkey legs
salt and pepper
cayenne
prepared **or** *French mustard*
butter

Remove the skin from the turkey, criss-cross with deep cuts. Sprinkle well with salt and pepper and a little cayenne, if required very hot. Spread with mustard, pressing well into the cuts and leave for several hours.

Grill for 8–12 minutes until crisp and brown, spread with small pieces of butter mixed with cayenne, and serve immediately.
Note Suitable for serving at a garden picnic or the turkey legs can be barbecued.

SERVES 2

POTTED VENISON

900 g/2 lb venison
50 ml/2 fl oz port wine
*100 g/4 oz butter **or** clarified dripping*
salt and pepper
clarified butter

Set the oven at 160°C/325°F/gas 3. Put the venison into a casserole with a close-fitting lid. Add the wine and butter or dripping, and season with salt and pepper. Cover the top of casserole with two or three thicknesses of greased paper, press the lid down tightly, and cook for about 2 hours. Drain well, chop finely, pound in a mortar until smooth, moistening the preparation gradually with the gravy, and pass it through a wire sieve. Add salt and pepper to taste. Press into small pots, and cover with clarified butter.

SERVES 6 TO 8

CELEBRATION PICNIC

devilled turkey legs

potted venison

walnut and celery mayonnaise

pressed beef

cheese bread plait

picnic cheesecake

port wine jelly

piped almond rings

PRESSED BEEF

salt brisket of beef
1 onion
1 carrot
½ turnip
bouquet garni
10 peppercorns
meat glaze

Weigh the meat. Wash it well, or if very salty soak for about 1 hour in cold water. Put into a saucepan and cover with cold water. Bring slowly to boiling point. Skim well. Cut the prepared vegetables into large pieces, add to the meat with the bouquet garni and peppercorns, and simmer gently, allowing 25 minutes per 450 g/1 lb and 25 minutes over.

Take the meat out, remove the bones and press between two boards or dishes until cold. Then brush over with meat glaze.

SERVES 6

'Bill of Fare for a picnic for 40 Persons.

A joint of cold roast beef, a joint of cold boiled beef, 2 ribs of lamb, 2 shoulders of lamb, 4 roast fowls, 2 roast ducks, 1 ham, 1 tongue, 2 veal-and-ham pies, 2 pigeon pies, 6 medium-sized lobsters, 1 piece of collared calf's head, 18 lettuces, 6 baskets of salad, 6 cucumbers.

Stewed fruit, well sweetened, 3 or 4 dozen plain pastry biscuits, 2 dozen fruit turnovers, 4 dozen cheesecakes, 2 cold cabinet puddings, 2 blancmanges, a few jam puffs, 1 large cold plum

ADVICE FROM
MRS BEETON

pudding, a few baskets of fresh fruit, 3 dozen plain biscuits, a piece of cheese, 6 lbs of butter, 4 quartern loaves, 3 dozen rolls, 6 loaves of tin bread, 2 plain plum cakes, 2 pound cakes, 2 sponge cakes, a tin of mixed biscuits, ½ lb of tea.

Things not to be forgotten at a picnic. A stick of horseradish, a bottle of mint sauce well corked, a bottle of salad dressing, a bottle of vinegar, made mustard, pepper, salt, good oil, and pounded sugar. If it can be managed, take a little ice. It is scarcely necessary to say that

plates, tumblers, wine-glasses, knives, forks and spoons must not be forgotten; as also teacups, and saucers, 3 or 4 teapots, some lump sugar, and milk. Take three corkscrews.

Beverages. – 3 dozen quart bottles of ale, ginger beer, soda water, and lemonade, of each 2 dozen bottles; 6 bottles of sherry, 6 bottles of claret, champagne, and any other light wine that may be preferred, and 2 bottles of brandy.'

Mrs Beeton
Book of Household Management, 1861

BAKED HAM LOAF

fat for greasing
100 g/4 oz browned breadcrumbs
225 g/8 oz ham, minced
100 g/4 oz corned beef, minced
15 ml/1 tbsp finely chopped parsley
5 ml/1 tsp grated lemon rind
1 large cooking apple, peeled, cored
and grated
50 g/2 oz sultanas
a pinch of allspice
a pinch of grated nutmeg
salt and pepper
2 eggs, beaten
milk

Well grease a loaf-tin and coat with browned breadcrumbs. Set the oven at 150°C/300°F/gas 2.

Mix the ham and corned beef with the parsley, lemon rind, breadcrumbs, apple, sultanas, spices and salt and pepper. Bind with the beaten eggs and a little milk if needed. Carefully put into the prepared loaf-tin and bake for about 40 minutes. Serve hot with gravy, or cold with salad.

SERVES 6

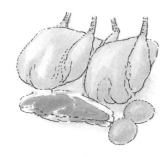

GROUSE PIE

2 grouse
350 g/12 oz rump steak
2 hard boiled eggs
2-3 bacon rashers
salt and pepper
300 ml/½ pint good stock
225 g/8 oz puff pastry

Set the oven at 220°C/425°F/gas 7.

Joint the birds and discard the vent-end parts of the backs, as these will impart a bitter flavour to the pie. Slice the steak thinly, slice eggs and cut the bacon into strips.

Line the bottom of a pie dish with pieces of seasoned meat, cover with a layer of grouse, add some bacon, egg and salt and pepper to taste. Repeat until dish is full. Add sufficient stock to three-quarters fill the pie dish, cover with puff pastry and bake for 1½–1¾ hours, reducing the oven temperature to 180°C/350°F/gas 4 after 15 minutes. Alternatively, cover the pastry with greaseproof paper so that the filling may cook a further 1¼–1½ hours. Glaze the pie 30 minutes before cooking is complete. Simmer the necks and trimmings of the birds in the remaining stock, strain, season and pour into the pie before serving.
Note Finely chopped mushrooms, parsley and shallots may be added to the pie, if liked.

SERVES 6 TO 8

LAMB CUTLETS
A LA MAYONNAISE

6 lamb cutlets
potted foie gras **or** *farce*
mayonnaise
aspic jelly **or** *gelatine*
radishes
chervil **or** *lettuce*
green salad

Braise or grill the lamb cutlets or
sauté in butter. Then press between
two plates with a weight on top
until cold. Trim the cutlets neatly,
making them all the same shape
and size if possible.

Coat one side with potted foie
gras or any other farce; be careful to
keep the cutlets lying one way up so

that they can be dished neatly.
Smooth the farce with a wet knife
and place on a wire rack over a
dish. Add to the mayonnaise a
little stiff aspic jelly or dissolved
gelatine which is beginning to set.
Carefully coat the cutlets with this
mixture. Garnish with tiny rounds
of radish (like berries) and one or
two leaves of chervil or lettuce. If a
very glossy finish is required, pour a
layer of cold, liquid aspic over the
top. Keep cold and serve with green
salad.

SERVES 6

TRAVELLERS' FARE

While wealthy Victorians amused themselves on their country estates, the prosperous middle-classes enjoyed day-trips to the countryside by train or horse-drawn carriage. Since it was difficult to find restaurants or provisions away from the towns, the midday meal was transported with the party. As long ago as the 1870s some of the railway companies offered luncheon hampers and three shillings purchased chicken, ham, salad, bread, cheese, butter and a bottle of wine in a sturdy, returnable wicker basket. Early picnic hampers often contained a tea pot and burner as well as cutlery, crockery and containers for food.

$\mathscr{S}$ALADS

Salads of all descriptions are perfect for picnics – they are light and nutritious, may be suited to any occasion and are easily transported. For best results with green salads, add dressings just before serving.

WALNUT AND CELERY MAYONNAISE

2–3 celery sticks, finely shredded
100 g/4 oz walnuts, coarsely chopped
salt and pepper
30 ml/2 tbsp thick mayonnaise
15 ml/1 tbsp double cream (optional)
watercress sprigs

Mix the celery and walnuts together, with a little salt and pepper to taste, and gradually add the mayonnaise and cream (if used). Pack the mixture into a container and place some watercress sprigs on top. Cover with a lid or foil for transporting.

SERVES 4

CHICKEN SALAD

1 small cooked boiling fowl **or**
remains of a cooked chicken **or** *turkey*
1 celery heart (optional)
1 large lettuce
10 ml/2 tsp caper vinegar
salt and pepper
150 ml/¼ pint mayonnaise
2 hard-boiled eggs
olives **or** *gherkins*
15 ml/1 tbsp capers

Cut the chicken into neat, small
pieces. Shred the celery and the
outer leaves of lettuce. Mix lightly
with the vinegar and a little salt
and pepper.

Pile into a container and coat
with the mayonnaise. Garnish with
lettuce leaves, slices of hard-boiled
egg, stoned olives or strips of
gherkins, and capers.

SERVES 6

GREEN PEA AND BEAN SALAD

1 garlic clove, halved
350 g/12 oz cooked green peas
350 g/12 oz cooked French beans, cut
in 2.5 cm/1 inch lengths
30–45 ml/2–3 tbsp French dressing
2 hard-boiled eggs, sliced
1 small beetroot, sliced
2.5 ml/½ tsp finely chopped parsley

Rub the inside of a china or glass
container with the cut side of the
garlic clove. Mix the peas and
beans with the dressing and put
into the container. Lay the slices of
hard-boiled egg and beetroot on top
and sprinkle with the parsley.
Cover with a lid or foil for
transporting.

SERVES 6

RUSSIAN SALAD

1 small cauliflower
75 g/3 oz peas
75 g/3 oz vegetables (carrot, turnip,
French beans)
3 potatoes
1 small cooked beetroot
2 tomatoes, peeled and sliced
aspic jelly
50 g/2 oz diced ham **or** *tongue*
50 g/2 oz cooked fish
(shrimps, prawns, lobster)
50 g/ 2 oz smoked salmon (optional)
3 gherkins
10 ml/2 tsp capers
a few lettuce leaves
mayonnaise
1 hard-boiled egg (white only)
6 stoned olives
6 anchovy fillets

Prepare and cook all the vegetables
(or use canned or bottled
vegetables). Drain them well.
Divide the cauliflower into small
sprigs, dice the other vegetables
except the peas and tomatoes.

Line a border mould with aspic
jelly and decorate it with a little of
the diced vegetables. Set layers of
vegetables, meat, fish and pickles
alternately with jelly in the mould;
do not use all the vegetables. When
set, turn out. Toss shredded lettuce
and the remaining vegetables in
mayonnaise and pile in the centre
of the mould. Garnish with egg
white, olives and anchovy fillets.

SERVES 6

POTATO SALAD

6 large new potatoes **or** *waxy old*
potatoes
French dressing
30 ml/2 tbsp chopped parsley
5 ml/1 tsp chopped mint
5 ml/1 tsp chopped chives **or** *spring*
onion
salt and pepper

Cook the potatoes until just soft, in
their skins. Peel and cut into dice
whilst still hot. Then mix
immediately with the dressing,
herbs and a little salt and pepper.

Pack into a container and cover
with a lid or foil when cold for
transporting.

SERVES 6

SAFELY PACKED

When deciding on a picnic menu, choose dishes that are reasonably easy to transport, and follow these basic tips:

✱ Pack any spillable items, such as salads, pasta dishes, and casseroles, into rigid containers with tightly fitting lids.

✱ Pack salad dressing separately in airtight, screw-topped bottles. Just before serving, shake vigorously and pour on to the salad.

✱ Wrap cold meats and fish in cling film or foil.

✱ Carry hot soups in wide-necked vacuum flasks.

✱ Transport tarts and quiches on sturdy plates covered with cling film or foil and packed inside a box or tin.

✱ Leave meat loaves, mousses and pâtés in the containers in which they were made.

✱ Wrap breads and sandwiches tightly in two layers of cling film.

✱ Carry cakes and biscuits in airtight tins or boxes.

✱ Transport bottles in a rigid container and surround with ice packs.

$\mathcal{S}$ANDWICHES

Sandwiches can be much more than a quick snack between meals. With interesting breads or rolls and varied fillings they can make a well-balanced meal that travels well and is adaptable to any season.

PRINCESS SANDWICHES

175 g/6 oz cooked chicken, finely chopped
75 g/3 oz cooked ham, finely chopped
15 ml/1 tbsp grated cheese
2 hard-boiled egg yolks
2.5 ml/½ tsp lemon juice
prepared mustard
salt and pepper
olive oil
thin slices of buttered white bread

Pound the chicken and ham in a mortar with the cheese and egg yolks, adding lemon juice, mustard, salt and pepper to taste, and sufficient oil to moisten the mixture. Spread on slices of bread and butter, press together well, trim neatly, and cut into required shapes.

SERVES 4 TO 6

THE PERFECT
SANDWICH

The sandwich is said to have been invented in 1764 by John Montague, the 4th Earl of Sandwich. During one of his 24-hour sessions at the gambling table, he asked his servant to bring him two slices of bread with a slice of beef between so that he would not have to leave the game.

For perfect sandwiches:

*** Always use bread that is 12–24 hours old (use rolls as fresh as possible) and chill for 30 minutes before slicing.

*** Soften butter before spreading and spread right up to the edges of each slice of bread.

*** Fill sandwiches generously and add salt and pepper to taste.

*** Press each sandwich well together and place a hand on top to hold firm; slip the knife between hand and sandwich and cut into the required shape.

*** Store in cling film or foil until needed. The best results are obtained when the sandwiches are made as near to the time of eating as possible.

SPORTSMAN'S SANDWICHES

Toast some 5mm/¼ inch thick slices of bread lightly, split them and butter the plain sides. On half of them lay thin slices of cold game, chicken, or meat, spread on a little tartare sauce seasoned with French mustard, and cover with the remaining slices of bread. Press together well, trim neatly, and cut into squares. Wrap them in lettuce leaves, and finally in cling film or foil.

SUGGESTED FILLINGS

Thin slices of cold roast beef, topped with a thin layer of horseradish sauce.

A slice of boiled ham spread with red tomato chutney.

Softened cream cheese mixed with canned crushed pineapple and finely chopped preserved ginger.

Thick slices of banana sprinkled with coarsely grated chocolate.

A layer of cottage cheese, covered with a layer of fresh strawberries or raspberries sprinkled with caster sugar.

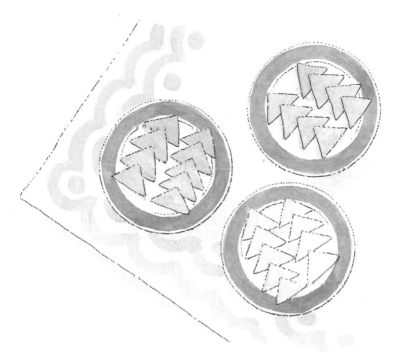

SAVOURY BUTTERS

Spread the slices of bread with savoury butters to complement the filling:

Anchovy – cream 100 g/4 oz butter well with 5 ml/1 tsp anchovy essence and season lightly with cayenne.

Green – cream 100g/4 oz butter well, then beat in 15–30 ml/ 1–2 tbsp finely chopped parsley, 15 ml/1 tbsp lemon juice, anchovy essence and salt and pepper to taste.

Mustard – cream 100 g/4 oz butter well, then mix in 5ml/1 tsp prepared mustard and a little salt.

$\mathscr{P}$UDDINGS

There is no reason why picnics should not include desserts that are as tempting as those at any other meal. Indeed, a delicious pudding, attractively presented, can turn an ordinary picnic into a special occasion.

PICNIC CHEESECAKE

BASE
75 g/3 oz butter
150 g/5 oz fine dry white breadcrumbs
50 g/2 oz caster sugar
7.5 ml/3 tsp ground cinnamon

FILLING
3 eggs, separated
100 g/4 oz caster sugar
375 g/13 oz full-fat soft cheese
grated rind and juice of 1 lemon
125 ml/4 fl oz soured cream
25 g/1 oz chopped mixed nuts
caster sugar and cinnamon for dusting
15 ml/1 tbsp butter

Set the oven at 180°C/350°F/gas 4. Make the base. Melt the butter in a frying pan and stir in the breadcrumbs. Cook over a gentle heat, stirring until the crumbs are golden. Remove from the heat, stir in the sugar and cinnamon and leave to cool.

Press about two-thirds of the crumbs over the base of a loose-bottomed 20 cm/8 inch cake tin. Reserve the remaining crumbs.

Beat the egg yolks in a bowl until liquid. Set aside 15 ml/1 tbsp of the sugar in a small bowl. Add the remaining sugar to the egg yolks, beating until creamy. Press the cheese through a sieve into the bowl, then work in lightly. Add the lemon rind and juice to the mixture with the cream.

In a clean, grease-free bowl, whisk the egg whites to soft peaks. Stir 30 ml/2 tbsp into the cheese mixture, then fold in the rest lightly. Turn the mixture gently on to the prepared base in the tin. Bake for 45 minutes.

Sprinkle the reserved crumbs and the nuts on top of the partially cooked cheesecake and return to the oven for 15 minutes more.

Meanwhile, mix the cinnamon with the reserved sugar. Remove

the cake from the oven and test that it is firm in the centre. Increase the oven temperature to 220°C/425°F/gas 7.

Sprinkle the cinnamon and sugar mixture over the top of the cheesecake and dot with the butter. Return the cheesecake to the oven for 2–4 minutes or until glazed on top. Cool in the tin, then cover the top with foil for transporting safely.

SERVES 8 TO 10

RED FRUIT SALAD

225 g/8 oz redcurrants
6 red plums, stoned and quartered
225 g/8 oz strawberries, hulled
225 g/8 oz raspberries, hulled
100 g/4 oz slice watermelon, seeded
and cubed

Using a pair of kitchen scissors, neatly snip the redcurrants into small bunches.

Combine the plums, strawberries, raspberries and watermelon in a large container. Lay the redcurrants on top.

Serve as soon as possible, with Greek yogurt or cream and some sugar, if liked.

SERVES 6

PORT WINE JELLY

600 ml/1 pint water
25 g/1 oz gelatine
50 g/2 oz caster sugar
30 ml/2 tbsp redcurrant jelly
300 ml/½ pint port wine
red food colouring

Put 60 ml/4 tbsp of the water in small bowl and sprinkle the gelatine on top. Stand the bowl over a saucepan of hot water and stir the gelatine until it has dissolved completely. Meanwhile heat the remaining water with the sugar and redcurrant jelly until these dissolve. Remove from the heat and stir in the gelatine. Add half the port wine and colour dark red with a few drops of colouring.

Strain through two thicknesses of muslin; add the remaining port wine. Pour into a wet mould and leave to set. Cover with foil for transporting.

SERVES 6

CUSTARD TART

250 ml/8 fl oz milk
2 eggs
50 g/2 oz caster sugar
pinch of grated nutmeg

SHORT CRUST PASTRY
100 g/4 oz plain flour
1.25 ml/¼ tsp salt
50 g/2 oz margarine (or half butter,
half lard)
flour for rolling out

Put an 18 cm/7 inch flan ring on a heavy baking sheet, or line an 18 cm/7 inch sandwich cake tin with foil. Set the oven at 190°C/ 375°F/ gas 5.

Make the pastry. Sift the flour and salt into a bowl, then rub in the margarine until the mixture resembles fine breadcrumbs. Add enough cold water to make a stiff dough. Press the dough together with your fingertips. Roll out on a lightly floured surface and use to line the flan ring or tin.

In a saucepan, bring the milk to just below boiling point. Put the eggs and caster sugar into a bowl, mix well, then stir in the scalded milk. Strain the mixture into the pastry case and sprinkle the top with grated nutmeg. Bake for 10 minutes.

Lower the oven temperature to 150°C/300°F/gas 2 and bake for 15–20 minutes more or until the custard is just set.

SERVES 4 TO 6

Cut the pieces of fruit to suit the hollows of the mould, dip each piece into cold liquid jelly and set in place around and on the jelly layer. Leave to set and cover carefully with a layer of clear jelly. Allow to set. Repeat, taking care that each layer of fruit is quite firm before adding a layer of jelly – otherwise the fruit may be 'floated' from its position. Fill the mould to the top. Cover with foil for transporting.

SERVES 6

FRUIT IN JELLY

900 ml/1½ pints very clear lemon jelly
pieces of fruit, such as sliced bananas,
halved grapes, stoned cherries, orange
segments and cubed pineapple

Rinse a jelly mould with cold water. Cover the bottom with a thin layer of cool jelly (about 3 mm/⅛ inch thick). Avoid the formation of bubbles in the jelly by tilting the mould and placing the jelly in spoonfuls in the bottom. Leave to set.

DECORATIVE
DESSERTS

When preparing puddings for a special picnic, choose plates and dishes that will look attractive. China and glass plates will travel just as well as plastic provided they are packed carefully. If necessary, transport fruit salads in plastic boxes, and moulded jellies in the containers in which they were made; then, when it is time to serve them, turn out into the pretty serving dish.

Take garnishes separately – for example, a few sprigs of washed, fresh mint for the top of a fruit salad, or some sliced strawberries or whole raspeberries for the top of a jelly or mousse. It is even possible to carry a bowl of chilled, whipped cream and a piping bag in order to decorate a treacle tart or a cheesecake with elaborate swirls.

$\mathscr{B}$READS AND SCONES

*Home-baked breads and scones are undoubtedly better
than shop-bought varieties, and add a special touch to a
picnic. Serve with pies, cold meats, cheese and pickles, or
slice for tasty sandwiches.*

CHEESE BREAD PLAIT

*fat for greasing
450 g/1 lb plain flour, warmed
5 ml/1 tsp salt
15 g/½ oz yeast
2.5 ml/½ tsp caster sugar
50 g/2 oz lard **or** margarine
75-100 g/3-4 oz cheese, grated
about 300 ml/½ pint warm milk
1 egg (optional)*

Grease a baking sheet. Mix the flour with the salt in a bowl. Cream the yeast with the sugar. Rub the fat into the flour and add the cheese. Mix with the yeast, milk and egg (if used) to a fairly soft, light dough. Beat until the mixture is smooth. Leave to stand in a warm place until doubled in volume.

Set the oven at 230°C/450°F/gas 8. Roll risen dough into two strips, each 25 cm/10 inches long and 13-15 cm/5-6 inches wide. Cut each strip almost to the top in three even-sized pieces and plait them together. Moisten and seal the ends neatly but firmly and put on the prepared baking sheet. Allow to prove for 10–15 minutes. Brush with beaten egg and bake for 20–30 minutes, reducing the oven temperature after the first 10 minutes to 200°C/400°F/gas 6.

MAKES TWO PLAITS

PICNIC ESSENTIALS

As well as all the food, the following are essential:

– plates, knives, forks, spoons, serving spoons, serving knives, wine glasses, tumblers or beakers, cups and saucers
– a bottle opener
– stoppers for unfinished bottles
– salt, pepper and mustard, and any other sauces and chutneys
– tea, coffee, a vacuum flask of boiling water, milk, sugar
– garnishes for food

– ice cubes in a wide-necked thermos flask
– linen or paper napkins
– damp flannels or towels to wipe sticky fingers
– ice packs to keep the food cool in transit
– waterproof sheeting and blankets to sit on, and a few cushions
– a pretty tablecloth on which to display the food
– insect repellant and antihistamine creams
– a rubbish bag

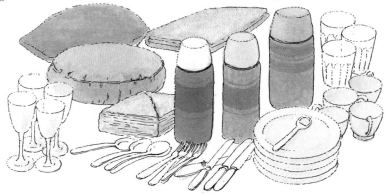

WHOLEMEAL BREAD

fat for greasing
1.4 kg/3 lb wholemeal flour
15 ml/1 tbsp salt
25 g/1 oz yeast
5 ml/1 tsp caster sugar
1 litre/1¾ pints warm water
50 g/2 oz lard, melted

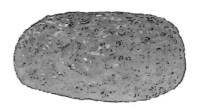

Mix the flour and salt in a large bowl. Cream the yeast with the sugar, add the warm water and melted fat, and mix with the flour to an elastic dough. Knead well until smooth, cover with a cloth, and set in a warm place to rise to double its volume – about 1 hour. When the dough is sufficiently risen it has a honeycombed appearance.

Set the oven at 230°C/450°F/ gas 8. Knead the dough again until, when the dough is cut, there are no large holes in it, but do not knead too heavily. Divide into four equal portions and put in warmed greased tins, making the tops round. Allow to prove for 20 minutes or until the dough is well up to the top of the tins. If the dough is over-proved, it will collapse and give heavy bread. Bake in the top of the oven for 10–15 minutes, then reduce the oven temperature to 190°C/375°F/ gas 5, baking in all for about 1 hour. When ready the loaves should have a hollow sound when tapped on the bottom, and should be well risen and nicely browned with a crisp crust.

MAKES FOUR 450g/1lb LOAVES

POTATO SCONES

*225 g/8 oz cold cooked potatoes,
sieved or mashed
15 g/½ oz margarine, melted
salt
about 75 g/3 oz plain flour*

Mix the potatoes with the
margarine and salt – the amount of
the latter depends on how much
salt has been used in cooking the
potatoes. The scones are very
tasteless unless there is some salt in
the mixture. Work in as much flour
as the paste will take up.

Roll the paste out very thinly on
a lightly floured surface. Cut into
rounds, using a 7.5 cm/3 inch
cutter, or triangles, and prick well
with a fork. Place on a moderately
hot griddle and cook for 3 minutes
on each side. Wrap in a clean tea-
towel and leave to cool.

MAKES 8 TO 10

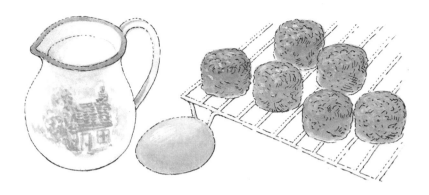

TREACLE SCONES

fat for greasing
200 g/7 oz plain flour
1.25 ml/¼ tsp salt
50 g/2 oz butter or margarine
15 g/½ oz caster sugar
2.5 ml/½ tsp ground cinnamon
2.5 ml/½ tbsp mixed spice
5 ml/1 tsp bicarbonate of soda
10 ml/2 tsp cream of tartar
15 ml/1 tbsp black treacle
125 ml/4½ fl oz fresh milk
flour for rolling out
milk or beaten egg for glazing
(optional)

Grease a baking sheet. Set the oven at 220°C/425°F/gas 7.

Sift together the flour and salt into a large bowl. Rub the fat into the flour until the mixture resembles fine breadcrumbs. Sift in the sugar, spices and dry raising agents and mix well. Add the treacle with the milk and mix lightly and quickly to form a soft, slightly sticky dough. Knead very lightly until smooth.

Roll out the dough on a floured surface to about 2.5 cm/1 inch thickness and cut into rounds using a 2.5 cm/1 inch cutter. Re-roll the trimmings and re-cut.

Put the scones on the prepared baking sheet and brush the tops with milk or beaten egg, if liked. Bake for 7–10 minutes until well risen and golden brown. Cool on a wire rack so that the scones are crisp on the outside.

MAKES 10 TO 12

CHEESE WHIRLS

SUMMER PICNIC

brawn

boiled ham

wholemeal bread

princess sandwiches

red fruit salad

apple and walnut flapjacks

countess spice cake

Set the oven at 220°C/425°F/gas 7.

Add 50–75g/2–3 oz grated cheese to the basic scone mixture (see Treacle Scones).

Roll out the dough into an oblong shape. Spread with the cheese and roll up like a Swiss Roll. Cut into slices and lay on greased baking sheets with the cut-side uppermost. Brush with milk or egg. If any cheese is left over, sprinkle it on and bake for 10–15 minutes.

MAKES 10 TO 12

41

*C*AKES AND BISCUITS

Lunch or tea-time picnics are always improved if there are home-made cakes and biscuits on the menu. Chunky gingerbreads and flapjacks are ideal for hungry children and lighter biscuits and cakes suit any elegant occasion.

A ROYAL PICNIC

'At length, at about three, we stopped and lunched at a place called Dalcronachie, looking up a glen towards Loch Loch – on a high bank overhanging the Tilt. Looking back the view was very fine; so, while the things were being unpacked for lunch, we sketched. We brought our own luncheon and the remainder was as usual given to the men, but this time there were a great many to feed.

'We walked to a little hollow immediately above the Dhu Loch, and at about half past three seated ourselves there and had some very welcome luncheon.'

Extracts from *Journal of Our Life in the Highlands 1848-1865* by Queen Victoria

Sift the flour, bicarbonate of soda, salt and spices into a bowl. Add the sugar. Heat the treacle, syrup and butter or margarine gently in a saucepan until the fat has melted.

Stir the melted ingredients thoroughly into the dry ingredients, then beat in the eggs. Stir in the ginger wine and grated carrot.

Pour into the prepared tin and bake for 20 minutes, then reduce the oven temperature to 160°C/325°F/gas 3 for a further 25–30 minutes, until firm to the touch. Cool on a wire rack.

MAKES ONE 20 cm/8 inch CAKE

MOIST GINGERBREAD

fat for greasing
200 g/7 oz plain flour
5 ml/1 tsp bicarbonate of soda
1.25 ml/¼ tsp salt
10 ml/2 tsp ground cinnamon
10 ml/2 tsp ground ginger
75 g/3 oz soft dark brown sugar
100 ml/3½ fl oz black treacle
100 ml/3½ fl oz golden syrup
150 g/5 oz butter **or** *margarine*
2 eggs, beaten
30 ml/2 tbsp ginger wine
1 carrot, grated

Line and grease a 20 cm/8 inch square tin. Set the oven at 180°C/350°F/gas 4.

COUNTESS SPICE CAKE

fat for greasing
100 g/4 oz plain flour
100 g/4 oz cornflour
2.5 ml/½ tsp ground ginger
3.75 ml/¾ tsp ground nutmeg
3.75 ml/¾ tsp ground cinnamon
1.25 ml/¼ tsp salt
75 g/3 oz margarine
10 ml/2 tsp baking powder
75 g/3 oz caster sugar
2 small eggs
about 125 ml/4½ fl oz milk
50 g/2 oz currants
50 g/2 oz seedless raisins

Line and grease a 15 cm/6 inch cake tin. Set the oven at 180°C/ 350°F/gas 4.

Mix the flour, cornflour, spices and salt in a mixing bowl. Rub in the margarine until the mixture resembles fine breadcrumbs. Add the baking powder and sugar.

In a bowl, beat the eggs with 50 ml/2 fl oz of the milk and stir into the flour mixture. Add more milk, if necessary, to give a consistency which just drops off the end of wooden spoon. Stir in the currants and raisins.

Spoon the mixture into the prepared cake tin and bake for 1–1½ hours or until cooked through. Cool on a wire rack.

MAKES ONE 15 cm/6 inch CAKE

APPLE AND WALNUT FLAPJACKS

fat for greasing
75 g/3 oz margarine
75 g/3 oz soft light brown sugar
30 ml/2 tbsp clear honey
2 tart eating apples, peeled, cored and diced
100 g/4 oz walnuts, chopped
50 g/2 oz raisins
100 g/4 oz rolled oats

Grease a 28 × 18 cm/11 × 7 inch baking tin. Set the oven at 160°C/325°F/gas 3. Melt the margarine with the sugar and honey in a large saucepan over a low heat. Stir the mixture occasionally.

Off the heat, add the apples, walnuts and raisins to the melted mixture. Stir well, then add the oats and mix thoroughly. Press the mixture into the prepared tin and bake for 25 minutes, or until golden brown and firm.

Leave the flapjacks to cool in the tin, cutting them into fingers while still warm.

MAKES ABOUT 20

CRISP CRACKERS

fat for greasing
225 g/8 oz plain flour
2.5 ml/½ tsp salt
about 100 ml/3½ fl oz milk
1 egg yolk, beaten

Grease two baking sheets. Set the oven at 180°C/350°F/gas 4. Sift the flour and salt into a bowl, then make a well in the middle and add about half the milk. Add the egg yolk to the milk and gradually work in the flour to make a firm dough, adding more milk as necessary.

Turn the dough out on to a lightly floured surface and knead it briefly until it is perfectly smooth. Divide the piece of dough in half and wrap one piece in cling film to prevent it from drying out while you roll out the other piece.

Roll out the dough very thinly and use a 7.5 cm/3 inch round cutter to stamp out the crackers. Gather up the trimmings and re-roll them. Place the crackers on the prepared baking sheets and bake them for 12–18 minutes, until they are golden. Transfer the crackers to a wire rack to cool.

MAKES ABOUT 24

RINKS

For celebratory picnics the hamper must include cocktails,
wines, punches or champagne. For everyday occasions
take chilled bottles of lemonade and fruit juices and keep
cold by surrounding with plenty of ice packs.

GINGER BEER

1 lemon
275 g/10 oz caster sugar
15 g/½ oz ginger root, bruised
2.5 ml/½ tsp cream of tartar
2.8 litres/5 pints boiling water
10 ml/2 tsp brewers' yeast

Remove the rind of the lemon as
thinly as possible, strip off every
particle of white pith, and cut the
lemon into thin slices, discarding
the pips.

Put the sliced lemon into a bowl
with the sugar, ginger, and cream
of tartar, and pour in the boiling
water. Leave it to stand until luke-
warm, then stir in the yeast and
leave the bowl in a moderately
warm place for 24 hours.

Skim the yeast off the top, and
strain the ginger beer carefully from
the sediment. Bottle and tie the
corks down securely. In two days it
will be ready to drink.

MAKES ABOUT
2.8 litres/5 pints

MULLED WINE

300 ml/½ pint water
6 cloves
7 g/¼ oz cinnamon stick, bruised
nutmeg
thinly pared rind of ½ lemon
900 ml/1½ pints claret
caster sugar

Put the water in a saucepan and heat gently. Stir in the cloves, cinnamon, a grate of nutmeg and the lemon rind. Bring to the boil and cook for 10 minutes. Strain off the liquid into a bowl and add the wine. Sweeten to taste. Return the liquid to the pan and make hot without boiling. Serve at once or pour into a vacuum flask.

SERVES 6

BACCHUS CUP

½ bottle of champagne
300 ml/½ pint sherry
75 ml/3 fl oz brandy
30 ml/2 tbsp noyeau
15 ml/1 tbsp caster sugar
a few balm leaves
ice cubes
500 ml/17 fl oz soda water

Put the champagne, sherry, brandy, noyeau, sugar and balm leaves into a jug. Leave it to stand for a few minutes, then add some ice cubes and the soda water. Serve at once.
Note This cup cannot be prepared in advance so is only suitable for serving at a picnic in your garden.

SERVES 6 TO 8

WELL CHILLED

Ice was an essential ingredient in the making of Victorian moulded puddings and ice creams. It was gathered from rivers and lakes in the winter and stored in ice houses or pits, but town-dwellers usually bought their ice direct from the fishmonger or ice merchant. The earliest refrigerators were shelved cupboards or chests with a metal-lined compartment where the blocks of ice, wrapped in sacking or blankets, were placed. If ice was to be included among provisions for a picnic, and Mrs Beeton recommended that a little should be, it was similarly wrapped and placed in a waterproof container.

$\mathscr{I}$NDEX